We are all
beautiful
and
unique!

♡ Megan
DeSmith

DEDICATION

This book is dedicated to my amazing sons, Bronx and Shai.

Thank you for always teaching me
to find the beauty in everyone's differences,
to never give up, and to love everyone!

Love,

Mom

THE AUTHOR

Megan DeJarnett is an author, speaker and advocate. At the age of two, she was diagnosed with a terminal disease called Spinal Muscular Atrophy (SMA), which has had her in an electric wheelchair ever since. Throughout her life, Megan has been placed in unique situations and has had to overcome many challenges. However, she didn't think too much about her differences until she became the mother of a child with special needs. Megan found herself frequently having to answer questions about their differences. This birthed a passion in Megan, and now she has dedicated her life to teaching about how everyone is unique. Her message is clear and her mission will carry on until everyone believes there is "No Such Thing as Normal"!

Megan lives in Tennessee with her husband and two amazing children.

Megan, Jake, Bronx and Shai

Check out her website at: www.nosuchthing.co

Learn more about Spinal Muscular Atrophy (SMA) at: www.curesma.org

THE MOVEMENT

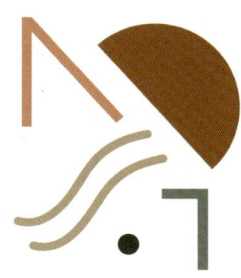

No Such Thing is a company whose mission is to "redefine purpose by removing labels". Their passion is for disability advocacy, with the goal to instill dignity and respect for all people, no matter their differences or abilities.

WRITER MEGAN DEJARNETT
ILLUSTRATOR CAILYN MATLEY
GRAPHIC DESIGNER MEAGHAN MITCHELL, CREATED

ORDERING INFORMATION AND DETAILS, CONTACT INFO@NOSUCHTHING.CO

Print ISBN: 978-0-578-64653-4

IN PARTNERSHIP WITH

wearecreated.co

no such thing as NORMAL

"Shane, I heard you have a new girl in your class at school."

"Yeah, she just moved here last week," Shane answered as he and his big brother, Brody, ate pancakes together.

"Well, what's she like?" asked their mom.

"She's nice, but she kind of talks funny," Shane said.

Brody made a silly face and asked,
"Funny? How?"
"I don't know," Shane shrugged.
"I don't think she's normal."
"Not normal, huh?" their mom asked
with a gentle smile. "Well boys, there's
no such thing as normal."

After breakfast, Shane, Brody and their mom headed to the library to return some books. When they arrived, their mom asked, "Boys, do you see those kids over there? Do you notice how they don't look the same?"

"Yeah," Brody answered. "That boy has brown hair and it's curly!"
"Different than yours, isn't it?" their mom pointed out.
"Oh, and that girl has red hair and spots on her face," Shane noticed.
With a little chuckle their mom said, "Those 'spots' are called freckles."
"Freckles? Wait, I don't have any freckles!" Brody made another funny face trying to look at his own nose.
Their mom reminded them, "Well, we are all made unique, and there's no such thing as normal."

On their way to the park, the boys noticed a man
walking with his dog.
"Mom, look!" Shane exclaimed. "That's a really
cool dog over there!"

The boys and their mom made their way over
to the man and his dog.
"Excuse me, sir, we really like your dog!"
Shane shared.
"Hello there. Thank you very much!
This is Max and he's my guide dog,"
the man said kindly.

"What's a guide dog?" asked Brody, looking
a little confused.

"A guide dog helps lead me because I'm blind,"
the man answered. "What's blind?" asked Brody.
"Blind means I cannot see," explained
the man. "But did you boys notice the birds
over there singing?"
"Wow! How did you hear that all the
way over there?"
"Even though I can't see, I can hear really
well," the man said.

"Super hearing and a dog that helps you see?
That's not normal!" the boys said.
"Well, guys, there's no such thing as normal,"
the man said. Then he walked away, whistling
along with the birds.

While they were at the park, Shane noticed a girl playing all by herself. "Would you like to play?" Shane asked, but the girl looked away and did not answer.

Confused, Shane went to his mom and said, "That girl won't play with me. Why won't she look at me when I talk to her?"

Another mom sitting close by heard Shane and said, "Hi! I couldn't help but hear your question. That's my daughter. Her name is Anna, and she has autism."

"What's autism?" asked Shane.

"Well, everyone with autism is different in their own way. Anna sometimes likes to play all by herself. She isn't trying to be mean. She just has a unique way of playing. Want to know something special about Anna?" asked Anna's mom.

"Yes!" Shane said with excitement.

"Anna is a wonderful artist," Anna's mom shared, as she pulled a beautiful drawing out of her bag.

"She drew that? She is a great artist, but she doesn't play normal," Shane said.

"There's no such thing as normal," Anna's mom said as she gave the boys a wink.

Just as they sat down for lunch, the boys
noticed a family next to them.
"Mom, why are they moving their hands like
that?" Brody wondered out loud.
"Oh, that's called Sign Language. Anybody
can learn it, but it's a special language for
people who are deaf."
"What does deaf mean, Mom?" Brody asked.
"Deaf means they have trouble hearing so they
talk with their hands," his mom replied.

"Talking with your hands isn't normal," Shane started to say, but their waitress chimed in,
"Well, some people say the way I talk isn't normal. I have an accent because I'm from Norway, and I learned to talk in another language. I actually speak four languages!"

"Wow, that's not normal either!" Brody said with a silly giggle. "But I like it!"
The waitress with the pretty voice said, "Remember, there's no such thing as normal."

As the boys and their mom were checking out at the grocery store, the young man bagging their groceries asked how their day was going.

Shane noticed something a little different about him and asked, "Could I ask you a question?"

"Sure. What's on your mind?" the young man said.

"Why do you talk and look different than me and my brother?" Shane asked with a little hesitation.

"Well, I talk a little different and look a little different because I have Down syndrome."
"So you're not normal like me?" asked Brody.
"There really is no such thing as normal," answered the young man as he gave the boys a high five.

Their last stop of the day was a birthday party, and the boys
were excited to see all of their friends.
As they were playing at the party, they noticed a little boy
sitting alone and looking sad.
Shane and Brody didn't want him to feel left out so they
went to ask him what was wrong.
The little boy answered, "The other kids were making
fun of me because of my mouth."
"What's wrong with your mouth?" asked Brody.
"I have a cleft lip and palate. It makes my face not look normal,"
the boy said quietly.
Shane and Brody looked at each other and smiled.
"There's no such thing as normal," they said,
"and we think you're awesome!"

As the boys climbed into bed that night their mom said, "I saw what you did at the party today. I'm very proud of you both."

Shane looked at his mom and paused for a moment. "Mom, do some people say that you are not normal?" he asked.

"Well, I do get a lot of questions, but I love helping people understand that we are all different. And being different and unique is a great thing."

"Yeah!," the boys said, "and there is no such thing as normal!"

"You are absolutely right!" said their mom as she kissed their heads good night.

"There is NO such thing as normal."

LET'S TALK ABOUT...

These questions are here to help promote healthy conversations. Our desire at No Such Thing is to assist in bridging the gap between the differences in all people, to show us the beauty in all humans. We hope these are helpful and provoke positive thinking about ourselves and others no matter the similarities or differences we live with.

1. **WHAT IS SOMETHING UNIQUE OR SPECIAL ABOUT YOU?**

   Example: I wear glasses. I have a great sense of smell. I run really fast.

2. **WHAT IS ONE WAY YOU CAN HELP MAKE SOMEONE FEEL INCLUDED OR ACCEPTED IF THEY'RE FEELING LEFT OUT OR SAD?**

   Example: Invite them to eat lunch with us. Ask them if they'd like to play with me and my friends.

3. **WHAT IS A POLITE WAY TO ASK SOMEONE ABOUT THEIR DIFFERENCES?**

   Example: Why do you have a scar vs. what's wrong with your face? Can you tell me about... vs. what's wrong with you?

4. **WHAT ARE SOME GOOD THINGS ABOUT HAVING FRIENDS THAT ARE DIFFERENT THAN US?**

   Example: Other people have cool talents that I don't have!

5. WHY IS STARING NOT CARING?

Example: Staring can make others feel...

6. WHAT DOES 'NO SUCH THING AS NORMAL' MEAN TO YOU?

Example: To me, "No Such Thing as Normal" means...

OTHER GREAT TIPS!

1. PROMOTE INTERACTIONS

- Instead of teaching our children not to stare when they see someone different than them, let's encourage them to interact! Say hello, ask a question or simply smile!

2. GUIDE HEALTHY QUESTIONS

- Allow your children to ask questions! We believe allowing them to ask respectful questions will help them understand and feel more connected to others.
- We like to encourage asking questions such as "what's your name?" or "what do you like to do for fun?".

3. HIGHLIGHT SIMILARITIES

- Instead of focusing on what makes others different then us, focus on what we may have in common with them!